MW01100653

SURVIVING
TOXIC
TERRORISM

Steve Wohlberg

Remnant
Publications

Remnant Publications, Coldwater MI

Published by
Remnant Publications
649 East Chicago Road
Coldwater MI 49036
517-279-1304
www.remnantpublications.com

Cover design by Charles Lawson
Text design by Greg Solie • Altamont Graphics

ISBN 978-1-933291-69-7

SURVIVING
TOXIC
TERRORISM

How to Conquer Killer Chemicals
at War with Your Health

*Warning: This book is hazardous to unhealthy
habits. Yet its message could save your life.*

First, I'm not a doctor, so here is my disclaimer:
The information included in this book is for
educational purposes only and is neither intended nor
implied to be a substitute for professional medical advice.

That being said, here's our story. Our nightmare
began on a beautiful summer day in July of 2007. My
wife, Kristin, our three-year-old son, Seth, and I were
peacefully driving down northern California's scenic
Interstate Highway 101 among towering redwoods
when calamity struck like lightning from a clear blue
sky. "Something's wrong with Seth!" Kristin unexpectedly yelled after glancing backward at our child
who had fallen asleep in his car seat just moments
before. Immediately, I flashed a look behind me (I
was driving) and was shocked to see our little boy
convulsing and jerking. Panic gripped me. Quickly,
I pulled over, jumped into the back seat and shook
my son gently. "Seth? Are you having a bad dream?
Wake up!"

He couldn't—he was having his first seizure.

Months later, he had another one. Then another. After numerous tests, an EEG, and an MRI, Seth was finally diagnosed as having "benign rolandic epilepsy" and, based on the recommendation of three neurologists, was put on anti-seizure medication. "No known cause, no known cure," was the consistent conclusion we were given.

On the bright side, we were told that Seth would probably outgrow this disorder by his teens, and we were firmly advised to "keep him on medication" until then, or until he went two years without a seizure and his brain produced a normal EEG. This was explained to us as "standard protocol" for his condition.

So, nervously—all the while fearing the possibility of harmful side effects—I began inserting into my trusting child's open mouth a high-powered brain drug twice a day for the next 16 months.

Things went reasonably well for about a year except for three unusual occurrences. First, Seth's breath smelled like rotten flesh every morning, which seemed highly abnormal in a child. Second, his sleeping patterns became increasingly erratic, causing him to jerk and bounce all over the bed each night. Third, my wife and I often watched wide-eyed many nights as Seth would wake up and do weird things – such as contort his lips, mutter nonsense, cry uncontrollably, and wave his hands wildly near his ears as if he were being tormented by some unseen substance within his brain. We labeled these bizarre occurrences "night events," and even recorded one on video. "It's nothing to worry about," our neurologist told us, "and they have nothing to do with the medication."

In retrospect, we think he was wrong.

Then in October 2009 Seth had four more seizures—while on medication. Frantically, we drove him to Sacred Heart Children's Hospital in Spokane, Washington, for another EEG. "His brain activity is quite busy," reported the neurologist who read the report, "and he is not far away from having more serious seizures." Nevertheless, the official diagnosis remained the same: "benign rolandic epilepsy...no known cause, no known cure." "You should increase his medication," our neurologist frankly informed us.

This troubled me greatly.

My Search for a Cause

As In the midst of my turmoil, floating up from somewhere deep within hazy memories was an ancient Bible passage that says, "the curse causeless shall not come" (Proverbs 26:2). *There must be a cause to Seth's seizures,* I thought to myself, *and a solution.* "Dear God," I found myself praying from the depths of my soul, "Please help me to discover *why* Seth is having these awful seizures, and how to reverse this condition! In Jesus' name, Amen." This was possibly the most sincere prayer I have prayed in my entire life.

The full story is too lengthy to tell here; but in a nutshell, after that prayer, I began doing my own homework. After typing in "causes of seizures" on the Internet, and after hours of research, I discovered that seizures *can sometimes* be caused by poisonous substances in the brain. On Wednesday night, October 14, 2009, Seth convulsed again, and the next day I faced an awful dilemma. *Should I fly to Bend, Oregon, tomorrow for a weekend speaking appointment* (I travel frequently and give seminars on a variety of Bible topics) *or stay home with Kristin and Seth?* I was confused and tormented. I didn't want to leave Kristin alone with a seizure-active child, but my seminar was pending. People were expecting me and depending on me.

Finally, on Thursday night I prayed. "Lord, if Seth has another seizure tonight, I'm not going." Providentially, he didn't. So, I left, and I'm glad I did. For it was there in Bend, Oregon, that I met a nutritionist who recommended a natural product called "PCA-Rx" that may be able to gently remove heavy metals from the body. *

Hmm ... I don't know about this ... should I give this to Seth? After purchasing a bottle, and then consulting with a sympathetic doctor friend who recognized each ingredient listed on the label, I decided

---

*   These statements have not been evaluated by the Food and Drug Administration. This product is not intended to diagnose, treat, cure, or prevent any disease.

to give it a try. I remember the exact date when we first sprayed PCA-Rx into Seth's mouth—October 29, 2009.

Amazingly, four nights later, on November 1, something unusual happened. With Seth lying asleep right next to me, I was praying in our bedroom. Suddenly, light seemed to fill my heart, and a vivid sense of peace flowed into me. That night, *for the first time in a long time,* Seth slept peacefully all night in one place without jerking about wildly during sleep.

Something is changing, I thought to myself.

I was right.

Discovering the Real Culprit: Heavy Metals

Shortly thereafter, during an intense conversation with a dentist friend of mine about environmental "toxins" and their adverse effects upon one's health, Kristin and I learned about the highly specialized work of Dr. Jon Mundall—a full-fledged MD who graduated from Loma Linda University and who specializes in clinical toxicology. To my pleasant surprise, I learned that Dr. Mundall operated his "Liberty Clinic" not far from our home in Priest River, Idaho. Speaking by phone, we scheduled our first visit for December 4, 2009. Upon arriving at his Spokane, Washington, office, not only did Dr. Mundall adamantly disagree with the "no cause, no cure, keep Seth on medication" advice that we had so often received, but he did what none of the neurologists I had spoken to even suggested, which was to recommend an analysis of Seth's vitamin, mineral, and heavy metal levels. During that first visit, he took samples of Seth's hair, blood, and urine, and then he sent them to the Doctor's Data Laboratory in Chicago.

The results shocked us, but they confirmed my growing suspicions based on my research. Seth's body was *loaded with heavy metals like arsenic, uranium, cadmium, lead, cesium, antimony, barium, and a host of others poisons.* "These are neurotoxins," Dr. Mundall informed us. "The combination is especially bad. They can definitely cause seizures."

Our new course was confirmed: "detoxification."

In the weeks that followed we continued using PCA-Rx, plus we added "Chelation therapy" properly prescribed by Dr. Mundall. We also began supplementing Seth's diet with vitamins and minerals targeting his nerves and brain. On January 27, 2010, after following a carefully scheduled weaning process, we took the next big step. Contrary to the prevailing opinions of nearly every neurologist we had spoken to, *we took Seth entirely off his anti-seizure medication.*

The next three nights were rough. Each night, nearly one hour after falling asleep, Seth had another strange "night event" where he would wake up, cry uncontrollably, wave his hands near his ears, and roll around wildly. Temptation pressed hard upon us. *This is the result of taking Seth off the medicine. We should put him back on right away.* But, with Dr. Mundall's firm encouragement, we kept a steady course.

A week later temptation struck hard again when Seth had two more seizures back to back. "Hold the line," Dr. Mundall persisted. "These are side effects of *getting off the drug,* not a reason to go back." It was difficult, but we held on.

Our persistence was rewarded.

More Progress

In the weeks that followed, those bizarre "night events" *ceased entirely* and Seth's sleeping patterns improved steadily. Then came the kicker. On February 2, 2010, we returned to Sacred Heart Children's Hospital in Spokane, Washington, for a follow-up EEG after the one in October. Three weeks later a neurologist (not Dr. Mundall) reported the results to our family pediatrician: Seth's brain activity had significantly changed for the better, and he *no longer* had "benign rolandic epilepsy." Praise God!

As I write this (it's now November 2010), Seth remains off all medication, no longer has "night events," and sleeps peacefully almost every night. I would be lying if I said there haven't been any bumps along the road, but based on the big picture, *Kristin and I know we are on the right track,* and I can't tell you what a relief this has been to our family.

Going Public with Our Story

Others need this information, was a pressing conviction that grew in my heart and finally compelled me to put our story into writing. Now let me clarify something. I'm neither against doctors (Dr. Mundall *is* a doctor), nor am I angry with the neurologists I had spoken to. Nevertheless, this trying experience has taught our family that even sincere medical professionals can sometimes miss the boat by: 1) not searching for the underlying cause of a disease, and 2) by being clueless about how to correct it. In Seth's case, a powerful brain drug was consistently recommended, but there was a better, more natural way.

In April of 2010, I finally went public with the details of our family's journey in an article entitled, *No Cause, No Cure?* that I emailed to my White Horse Media e-news list of nearly 7,000 recipients. The response was phenomenal! *Hundreds wrote back sharing personal stories of mysterious illnesses and seizures, and requesting more information.* "How did your little boy get so much lead, arsenic, cadmium, and uranium in his body?" was the most common question I was asked.

I'll answer that question shortly.

But first, I'll increase the mystery by saying that in June of 2010 our entire family (me, Kristin, Seth, and our two-year-old daughter, Abby) went back to Dr. Mundall's clinic to be tested for heavy metals. As a 51-year-old who grew up in Los Angeles,

I was quite interested to see what chemicals might lurk inside my head too. *Snip, snip, snip,* went Dr. Jon Mundall with his scissors. After placing hair strands from each of our heads into miniature zip-loc bags, he sent them to Doctor's Data.

Four weeks later, my results came in. "Elevated levels of lead, cadmium, arsenic, and uranium"—the same substances we discovered in Seth. What about little Abby? Are you ready for this? *Same thing.* She's loaded. In fact, Abby turned out to be the most toxic member of our family!

How is this possible?

It's time to answer that question.

More Eye-opening Information

Throughout the last year, starting in October of 2009 when Seth had four seizures and a highly erratic EEG, I have done a lot of research about toxic chemicals in the environment and their possible connection to increasingly common woes like seizures, autism, Alzheimer's, Parkinson's, multiple sclerosis, and cancer. In my earnest quest for information, I discovered these eye-opening books:

- *Detoxify or Die,* by Sherry Rogers, M.D.

- *Invisible Killers: The Truth about Environmental Genocide,* by Rik Deitsch & Stewart Lonkey, M.D.

- *Excitotoxins: The Taste That Kills,* by Russell L. Blaylock, M.D.

- *The Hundred-year Lie: How to Protect Yourself from the Chemicals That Are Destroying Your Health*, by Randall Fitzgerald.

- *Slow Death by Rubber Duck: The Secret Danger of Everyday Things*, by Rick Smith and Bruce Lourie.

Personally, I think it would be wise of you to take a look at these books. Read the "customer reviews" on amazon.com. For the record, I'm not saying I agree with every line in each book, but overall, they are quite credible. "Where did your boy get all those poisons?" Now I know. Simply by breathing, eating, living in our home, and playing with toys most kids play with. In other words, from twenty-first-century air, water, soil, supermarkets, and even from the personal care products we use everyday day like shampoo, conditioner, soap, and toothpaste.

It's common knowledge that fish—both saltwater and fresh—are often loaded with mercury. Unfortunately, their slimy bodies aren't the only ones contaminated. Ours have been invaded, too. The fact is, whether we realize it or not, you and I now have the unfortunate privilege of being official members of *the most toxic generation in the history of the world.* We're all victims. There's no escaping it.

As a result of my family's emotional saga, White Horse Media (the Christian TV ministry I direct) has recently launched a "Surviving Toxic Terrorism" zone on our website (see the link at the end of this book). Take a look. Click around. Read a few articles. Watch some video clips. Be enlightened. *Be warned.*

One link goes to a series of articles published in *The Seattle Times* called "Fear in the Fields: How Hazardous Waste Becomes Fertilizer." The lead paragraph reports:

> A *Seattle Times* investigation found that, across the nation, industrial wastes laden with heavy metals and other dangerous materials are being used as fertilizer and spread over farmland. The process, which is legal, saves dirty industries the high costs of disposing of hazardous wastes. *The Seattle Times*, July 3–4, 1997

In his book *Fateful Harvest*, Pulitzer Prize finalist Duff Wilson first investigates, and then documents, this largely secretive and dangerous practice. As unbelievable as it sounds—it's happening. Across North America hundreds of large industrial and chemical companies, such as Big Steel, Big Aluminum, and Big Coal, are now saving Big Bucks by disposing billions of tons of poisonous toxic wastes—not by sending them to landfills, which they should be doing, but by cost effectively reclassifying them as "products" that aren't regulated by the EPA, and then by selling them as "bulk soil amendments" to fertilizer companies.

These toxins then enter farming soils.

Then they enter the plants and food chain.

Then they enter *you and me.*

It's a toxic trade, and most farmers don't even know it is happening. Yet it's a fact. Poisonous wastes *are* silently seeping from big industry onto railcars, into fertilizer companies, and then onto farmland, gardens, and crops like potatoes, corn, wheat, and soybeans. Unknowingly, when we innocently purchase produce from our local supermarket, these deadly chemicals (which don't appear on *any* labels) often slip silently into *our bodies and those of our kids.* Outrageous, isn't it? For proof, *read Wilson's book.*

Toxic Terrorism

On July 3, 2010, I spoke about toxic terrorism in Chewelah, Washington, not far from our home in northern Idaho. "Here's my story," said a woman after hearing my talk, "I'm a farmer, and some time ago I visited another farmer in Rosalia, Washington, who farms thousands of acres of wheat. I noticed that there were no gophers on his land. 'What's your secret?' I asked my friend. His response amazed me. 'My soil contains so many chemicals that no gopher lives here.' Then he added, 'There's not even a worm on my land.' That's when the lights went on in my head about what's happening."

Dumfounded, I asked this lady, "What happens to all that wheat? Is it harvested to feed animals?" "No," she quickly retorted, "It goes into the whole wheat bread we purchase at the market." How frightening! I can't help but wonder whether this might contribute to increasingly common "wheat intolerances."

My wife and I now make our own bread from organic wheat.

"Ten Americans": A Must-see Presentation

In the "Surviving Toxic Terrorism" zone of our website, we have links to a fascinating series of video presentations called "Ten Americans" produced by the Environmental Working Group. Ken Cook, the president, is the featured speaker. *I recommend that you watch those videos.* At the beginning of Mr. Cook's presentation, he pleasantly explains how his organization chose ten random Americans, took samples of their blood, and then subjected those samples to rigorous testing. The result? In every person they found:

- 212 industrial chemicals and pesticides
- 47 well-known consumer product ingredients
- 134 chemicals that are known carcinogens

Mr. Cook's audience could scarcely believe their ears. Mr. Cook then inquired, "Where did these ten random Americans get all these poisonous chemicals?" Then he threw a curve ball. After describing how many dangerous chemicals there are in everyday air (especially in cities), he stumped his hearers by saying, "Not from the air." *What?* Next he mentioned the pollutants floating around in tap water.

"Not from the water," he continued. *What?!* Once more. Next he described the myriads of poisons found in soil, plants, grapes, strawberries, apples, etc. due to chemical agricultural farming practices. "But they didn't get them from their food," Mr. Cook explained.

How can this be?

His audience sat spellbound.

Pushing the remote advancer for his PowerPoint presentation, Mr. Cook then showed a photograph of an ultrasound peering inside a woman's body. "That's my son before his birth," Mr. Cook declared. "He was one of those ten Americans." He then explained that the ten Americans were all fetuses whose umbilical cord blood had been closely analyzed by specialists *before they were born.*

Get it?

Poisons like these are in all of us.

Like I said, you and I have the unfortunate privilege of being official members of the most toxic generation in the history of the world. Are these chemicals negatively affecting our health? *Click.* Mr. Cook pushed his button, and there appeared on the screen the innocent face of a young child who looked to me like a four-year-old. Below that face appeared this startling statistic:

57% increase in childhood brain cancer

It's enough to make one weep.

In July 2010 Medline Plus, a service of the U.S. National Library of Medicine and the National Institutes of Health, listed cancer as the third leading cause of death among children, ages 1–4, and as the second leading cause of death among children ages 5–14.[1] The U.S. Centers for Disease Control's (CDC) "Fourth National Report on Human Exposure to Environmental Chemicals" reiterates Ken Cook's research by stating that the "CDC has measured 212 chemicals in people's blood or urine—75 of which have never before been measured in the U.S. population."[2]

Like I said, we're all toxic.

If all of these chemicals were fluorescent, we'd glow in the dark.

Toxins *Can Kill*

Not long ago I spoke in a certain church about "Bible prophecy" and "these last days" and learned of a four-year-old boy who had just died. A few months earlier, from what I was told, this little guy appeared normal and healthy. Suddenly, he started having seizures. When doctors took a closer look, they were horrified to discover that the boy's brain was riddled with tumors. Within a short time, he was dead.

While the exact cause remains a mystery, I now know that toxins can cause tumors. Make no mistake about it: toxic terrorism is real, serious, and deadly. Check out these facts straight from the EPA:

1. **Mercury** impairs neurological development (especially in children) and damages the brain.[3] (c)

2. **Lead** affects practically all systems of the body, especially the central nervous system, kidney, and blood cells. It can cause convulsions, coma, and death.[4]

3. **Arsenic** has been linked to cancer of the lungs, bladder, skin, kidney, liver and prostate.[5]

4. **Uranium** damages the kidneys and increases risk of bone, lung, and liver cancers, plus blood diseases.[6]

5. **Cadmium** affects the heart and blood vessels, GI tract, nervous, urinary, reproductive and respiratory systems, and causes cancer.[7]

Unfortunately, this tiny list is just the proverbial tip of the iceberg. According to a series of articles published by *Scientific American* called, "Chemical Marketplace," there are more than 80,000 chemicals produced and used in U.S. alone![8] How many are carcinogenic? Only God knows.

What Does the Bible Say?

After discovering such sober facts about the extent of the chemical soup that surrounds us, I began to search God's Word to see if it made any predictions about an end-time toxic generation. Allow me to share some Bible verses. The prophet Isaiah predicted that eventually:

The earth mourns and fades away, The world languishes and fades away; The haughty people of the earth languish. Isaiah 24:4, emphasis added

This passage predicts that "the earth" itself would mourn, fade away, and languish. To me, this suggests an environmental crisis of the worst sort. Here's another one. The Lord told Isaiah:

The earth will grow old like a garment, *And those who dwell in it will die in like manner.* Isaiah 51:6, emphasis added

Similar to Isaiah 24:4, this passage describes "the earth" growing "old," but then it advances to "and those who dwell in it will die in like manner." In other words, as "the earth" grows old, its people will suffer death as a direct result of its aging. Again, this seems to fit with environmental pollution, poisons in the oceans, rivers, soil, and air, and their deadly, carcinogenic effects upon human health. Open your eyes. Untold numbers are perishing due to earth's toxic woes. And it's not just people. Have you heard about vanishing bee populations? Many theorize a toxic cause for their demise too.

The last book of the Bible also makes a startling prediction. The context is clearly "the end of days." Notice carefully:

> The nations were angry, and Your wrath has come, And the time of the dead, that they should be judged, And that You should reward Your servants the prophets and the saints, And those who fear Your name, small and great, *And should destroy those who destroy the earth.* Revelation 11:18, emphasis added

This apocalyptic prophecy informs us that at the sunset of human history, God Almighty will finally intervene—and His act will come at a time when misguided mankind is literally destroying His earth. Now, I'm no rabid environmentalist (although I deeply appreciate the planet our Creator made for us); but to me, these Bible predictions seem to pinpoint *our generation.*

The Prince of Poisons

Now here's the kicker. Revelation also warns:

> Woe to the inhabitants of the earth and the sea! *For the devil has come down to you,* having great wrath, because he knows that he has but a short time. Revelation 12:12, emphasis added

It's obvious that Big Chemical, Big Agriculture, Big Pharma, Big Politician, and even Big Government often yield to the temptation to become more interested in financial profit than human health. But is it possible that there is also a malicious force operating *invisibly* behind the scenes bent on polluting human bodies, controlling human minds, and destroying human souls? *The Bible says there is.* It is "the Devil and Satan, who deceives the whole world" (Revelation 12:9). *He* is the one behind human brutality, the destruction of the earth, and toxic terrorism.

Yes, Lucifer exists, and he is up to no good.

Let me clarify. I don't believe Satan himself is directly injecting millions of tons of formaldehyde, sulfur dioxide, dioxins, sodium laurel sulfate, PCBs, DDT, Agent Orange, and heavy metals like mercury, arsenic, lead, and uranium into human bodies, but I do believe he is working *invisibly behind the scenes* through chemicals and corporate profiteering to poison the human family. Just like he first spoke through a serpent in Eden, so today he works through agents (and agencies—even government ones) "to steal, and to kill, *and to destroy*" (John 10:10, emphasis added). "He was a murderer from the beginning," warned Jesus Christ.

He is a murderer today.

Surviving Toxic Terrorism

Thankfully, God still rules from in the heavens, and He is much stronger than "the poisoner." The more I research this topic, the more impressed I am at how the Great Physician is working to help humanity survive the deadly forces arrayed against us. Even though physical healing rarely happens instantly, during this past year (2010) my son's condition has greatly improved, and His smiling face brings joy to my heart everyday. "I had lead in my head!" Seth blurted out once with a boyish twinkle. With God's help, combined with healthy choices, I'm determined that my son will not become another cancer statistic. Or my wife. Or little Abby. Or me.

Let me clarify something else. When I speak of "toxic terrorism," I use the word "terrorism" because many of the invading chemicals we're exposed to literally *war against our bodies, immune systems, health, and minds—and consequently, against our relationship with God.* This reminds me of Halloween evening, 1938, when Orson Welles began narrating H.G. Wells' book, *The War of the Worlds,* to his unsuspecting radio audience.

"Hostile invaders have come from Mars," the announcer stated, "and have landed in New Jersey. The eerie creatures are marching forward rapidly, killing as they go. Great destruction is taking place!" Fear gripped the listeners who thought it was real. "Fake Radio War Strikes Terror across America!" ran newspaper headlines the next day.

Obviously, what happened in 1938 was just a story; but today's silent invasion of deadly pollutants into our lungs, GI tracts, livers, kidneys, blood and brains isn't. Again, the threat is real, as are the cancers, tumors, and frightening diseases often related to them. Is there anything we can do to protect ourselves? Thankfully, yes, there is. Although we can't escape the invasion entirely, there are still some solid principles, practices, and even some products that can help us avoid dying "before our time" (Ecclesiastes 7:17).

First Principle: We Should Value Our Bodies

The first principle is to realize that we are "fearfully and wonderfully made" (Psalm 139:13) by a Master Designer (God Himself) who created our bodies *with natural detoxification systems highly capable of eliminating poisons and fighting disease.* Each of us has an immune system, a liver, kidneys, a bowel, and permeable skin skillfully designed to remove waste and chemicals through bowel movements, urination, and perspiration. Have you ever wondered why, without deodorant, we stink? It's because our bodies are eliminating junk. In fact, your body is the best "detox aid" you've got, and just in case you haven't fully realized it yet—you only have one. If you ruin it, you're sunk. That's why it makes sense to value our bodies (even though they aren't perfect) and to strengthen them through wise choices.

Our Creator loves us and wants us to "be in health" (3 John 2). He hates to see His children suffer. Beyond this, He also knows that a healthy body leads to clearer thinking and an enhanced ability to both discern and do His will. Therefore, if we "love life," want to "see good days" (1 Peter 3:10), and desire a closer walk with God (see Genesis 6:9), then we do well to invest some time learning what is best for our bones, blood cells, muscles, minds and souls, and to make some sacrifices. If we're unwilling to do this, then even Almighty God can't protect us from sickness, sirens, paramedics, and hospitals. Eventually, we'll "pay the piper," "reap" what we have sown (see Galatians 6:7), and finally descend to an early grave with the letters "RIP" engraved above our bones.

That's reality, not *War of the Worlds* fiction.

Second Principle: Develop Healthy Habits

So what should we do? The answer is: develop healthy habits. Many doctors, nutritionists, and health professionals can enlighten us with credible information about the life-and-death importance of eating lots of fruits, vegetables, whole grains, nuts and seeds; exercising regularly; drinking lots of water; getting plenty of sunlight; and enough sleep. This is basic. These days, sadly, most Americans eat more "merchandise" than food. Have you ever really examined the ingredient lists on the labels of most packaged snacks? It's scary. Countless "snack delights" are actually "chemical frights."

One book I read recently stated that, from a nutritional standpoint, many multimillion-dollar "fast food" chains could properly be renamed McDeath, Murder King, Jack n' the Casket, Taco Hell, Crispy Grease, and KFC (Kidney Failure and Cancer). Whether this is overstated or not, fast food franchises are definitely not "health and wellness centers."

Even worse, regular fruits and veggies found in most grocery stores and supermarkets aren't entirely safe either. Large percentages are genetically modified or engineered. Even perfect looking peaches, plums, broccoli, and lettuce may be laden with pesticides, insecticides, herbicides, and fungicides, originating in bottles branded with "Poison," "Can be fatal if swallowed," and skulls and crossbones on their labels. Even more chemicals may then be added to help preserve their "color" and "freshness."

Honestly, buying "certified organic" isn't a bad idea, even if costs a bit more.

Neither is filtering our water.

I'm not trying to depress you, but these are facts. *We're at war with tasteless, odorless, invisible, and yet killer chemicals highly hazardous to our health.*

You deserve to be warned.

Third Principle: Nutritional Boosts

To make matters even worse (brace yourself), America's farming soils have become woefully deficient in vital minerals needed for optimal health. For shocking proof taken directly from the U.S. Department of Agriculture's website, Google the article "The Disappearance of Nutrients in America's Orchards" by Alex Jack. From 1975-2001, lemons lost 57.4% of their calcium; peaches lost 78% of their iron; bananas lost 57.4% of their Vitamin A; and cherries lost 30% of their Vitamin C. Thus, my third principle is that we do well to supplement our daily diets with nutrient-saturated "super foods" to supply the lack.

After months of research, here is a quick list of what I consider to be the crème of the crop: organic Aloe Vera, Spirulina, virgin coconut oil, sea vegetables, chia seeds, and sprouted seeds (my kids love sprouts!). Again, don't take my word for it—do your own homework. If you Google these natural jewels, you will discover that each is jam-packed with unique blends of vitamins, minerals, enzymes, amino acids, and antioxidants highly beneficial to our bodies. Plus (and I imagine you're ready for some "good news" by now), they are reasonably inexpensive and easy to obtain. "An apple a day keeps the doctor away" may have been true one hundred years ago, but not today. Again, farming soils are depleted, and trace minerals are often lacking. That's why each of our body's *50-100 trillion cells* craves an extra nutritional boost.

Fourth Principle: Credible Detox Aids

If I implement the above three principles, many wonder, *why do I need anything else?* My response is, perhaps you don't. Perhaps your body's inherent "detox power" is enough. But on the other hand, mercury, lead, arsenic, cadmium, and uranium are often tough to remove. Seth needed extra help, and you may too. Thus, my fourth principle is that, alongside principles one through three, additional detoxification efforts may be useful. Yes, I realize quackery exists, and that sensible caution is needed. But based on my research, these options are worth considering:

First, detox foods. Universally recognized are lemons, grapefruit, garlic, onions, cabbage, cilantro, and "Chlorella" (a nutrient-rich algae) which all have healing properties to help the body eliminate poisons. Drinking distilled water also helps cleanse the entire system. So does fasting from food one day a week.

Beyond these, my wife Kristin and I honestly believe that "PCA-Rx," developed by Maxam Nutraceutics, helped detoxify Seth (I have lab reports from Doctor's Data demonstrating PCA-Rx's ability to increase heavy metal excretion in urine). We also used "Chelation therapy" properly prescribed by Dr. Mundall. In my quest, I have also discovered the detox power of "activated charcoal" which is used daily in hospitals and even recommended by U.S. Poison Control Centers in emergency situations. Mixed with water in a drink, charcoal can safely sweep toxins right out of the GI tract. "Bentonite clay baths" also work wonders. Charcoal and clay are inexpensive and natural. Used properly, they can be highly effective in removing killer chemicals from our bodies.

Finally, in her book, *Detoxify or Die*, toxicology expert Dr. Sherry Rogers recommends "far infrared saunas" for super detoxification through sweating. Our family now has one of these saunas, and my wife and I use it regularly. A good infrared sauna isn't cheap; but if you can afford one, they're worth the price.

Here's one more word of advice. Solid science and clinical testing should back up all credible "detox" aids. *Seek the proof*. Paul's counsel is timely, "Test all things; hold fast what is good" (1 Thessalonians 5:21).

"Martians have invaded Planet Earth," narrated Orson Welles to a terrified radio audience on Halloween evening in 1938. Again, this was just a story. Unfortunately, today's chemical invasion into air, water, soil, food, and human bodies isn't—and it's life or death. Not only that, but if God doesn't intervene soon, humanity itself could be threatened with extinction due to toxic overload. While it may be impossible to completely escape exposure, we can limit our risk, if we are willing to do what it takes.

Heavenly Hope

"Jesus went about all Galilee," the Bible reports, "teaching in their synagogues, preaching the gospel of the kingdom, *and healing all kinds of sickness and all kinds of disease among the people*" (Matthew 4:23, emphasis added). How marvelous! In God's Book, Jesus Christ is presented not only as the Savior of souls, but as the Healer of bodies too. When I prayed about Seth, He answered. I know He did. You should pray too, and trust the promise, "He cares for you" (1 Peter 5:7).

That said, I'm also a realist. Despite our best efforts, we may get sick too. That's life—the way it is. Yet the Good Book is filled with encouraging promises pointing beyond dark times to a bright, immortal future. Describing "the great day of the Lord" when Jesus Christ returns, Paul promised:

> For the trumpet will sound, and the dead will be raised incorruptible, and we shall be changed. *For this corruptible must put on incorruption,* and this mortal must put on immortality. 1 Corinthians 15:51–54, emphasis added

Did you catch that? Being "changed" to "incorruption" and "immortality" means no more heart disease, cancer, strokes, high blood pressure, aching backs, crippling arthritis, or even wrinkled skin. Beyond this, even Planet Earth itself will be given a facelift. After God purifies our world by fire, and "the elements … melt with fervent heat" (2 Peter 3:10), John prophesied:

> I saw a new heaven and a new earth, for the first heaven and the first earth had passed away. … And God will wipe away every tear from their eyes; there shall be no more death, nor sorrow, nor crying. There shall be no more

pain, for the former things have passed away."
Then He who sat on the throne said, "Behold, I
make all things new." Revelation 21:1, 4, 5

No more death, sorrow, tears, or pain—doesn't
that sound nice? It does to me. Debilitating disease, corporate greed, frantic calls to 911, hospital
ERs, expensive coffins, funeral services and shat-
tered families will be a thing of the past. Not only
that, but the New Earth will also be 100% *toxin free*.
Hallelujah! To top it all off, "everlasting love" will
rule forever (see Jeremiah 31:3)—such love that led a
peace-loving Creator to visit our sinful earth, appear
as a baby in Bethlehem, grow up in Judea, heal the
sick in Galilee, and finally die on a splintery cross
in the shadow of Jerusalem for the sins of the whole
world (see 1 John 2:2). On Sunday morning, He
rose from the dead (see Matthew 28:7). At this very
moment, His heart yearns for us, His arms are out-
stretched to us, and His forgiveness is available; and
with it comes an eternal hope "beyond the river" in a
pollution-free world.

Two winters ago I took Seth sledding near a large
snow bank. "Daddy," he blurted out unexpectedly, "If
I fell and disappeared in that snow, you would just
leave me, right?" My response was immediate. "No
Seth, I would dig you out." "But what if you didn't
have a shovel?" he shot back. Again, my response was
immediate. "I would dig you out with my bare hands."

Two thousand years ago, essentially, Jesus Christ did just that when His gentle hands were spiked to a cross. He was reaching out to us, trying to dig us out of sin and eternal death. "Come to Me" (Matthew 11:28), is His call today.

Through His love, *you* can survive toxic terrorism. *You* can have a new body in the New Earth. I hope to see you there.

Need Help?

White Horse Media recommends the health resources developed by "Healing Leaves." For more information, visit www.healingleaves.com or call 1-877-691-5845.

End Notes

1   http://www.nlm.nih.gov/medlineplus/ency/article/001915.htm

2   http://www.cdc.gov/exposurereport/

3   http://www.epa.gov/mercury/effects.htm

4   http://www.epa.gov/iaq/lead.html

5   http://water.epa.gov/lawsregs/rulesregs/sdwa/arsenic/index.cfm

6   http://www.epa.gov/rpdweb00/radionuclides/uranium.html

7   http://www.atsdr.cdc.gov/substances/toxsubstance.asp?toxid=15

8   http://www.scientificamerican.com/article.cfm?id=the-chemical-marketplace-triclosan

**More Enlightening Resources from
Steve Wohlberg**

The Left Behind Deception

The Left Behind Deception (Spanish)

Perils of Harry Potter & Witchcraft

The Rapture Deception

Decoding the Mark of the Beast

Discovering the Lost Sabbath Truth

The Darkness of Twilight

**Remnant Publications
1-800-423-1319
www.remnantpublications.com**

**White Horse Media
1-800-782-4253
www.whitehorsemedia.com**